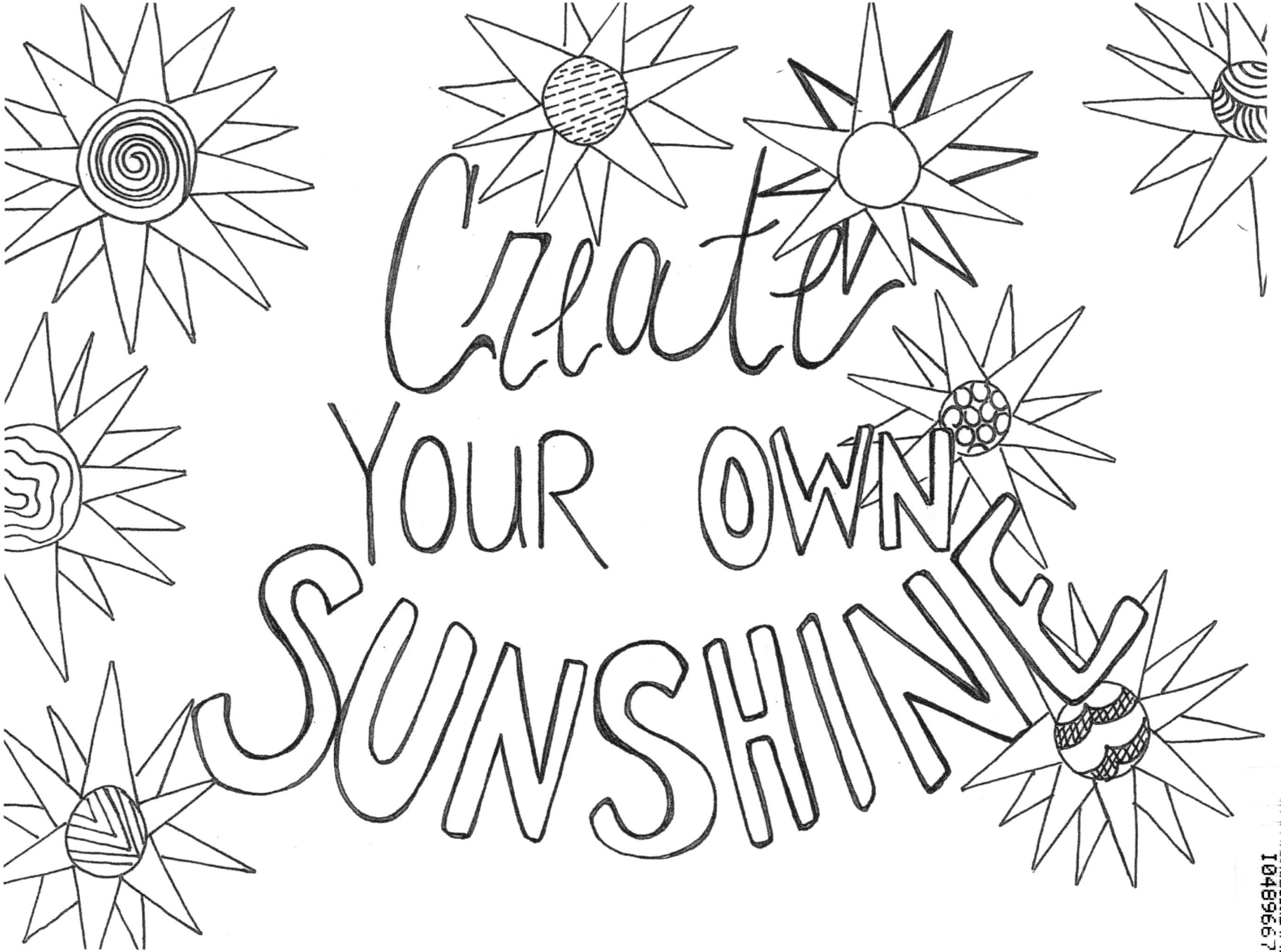

Create Your Own Sunshine

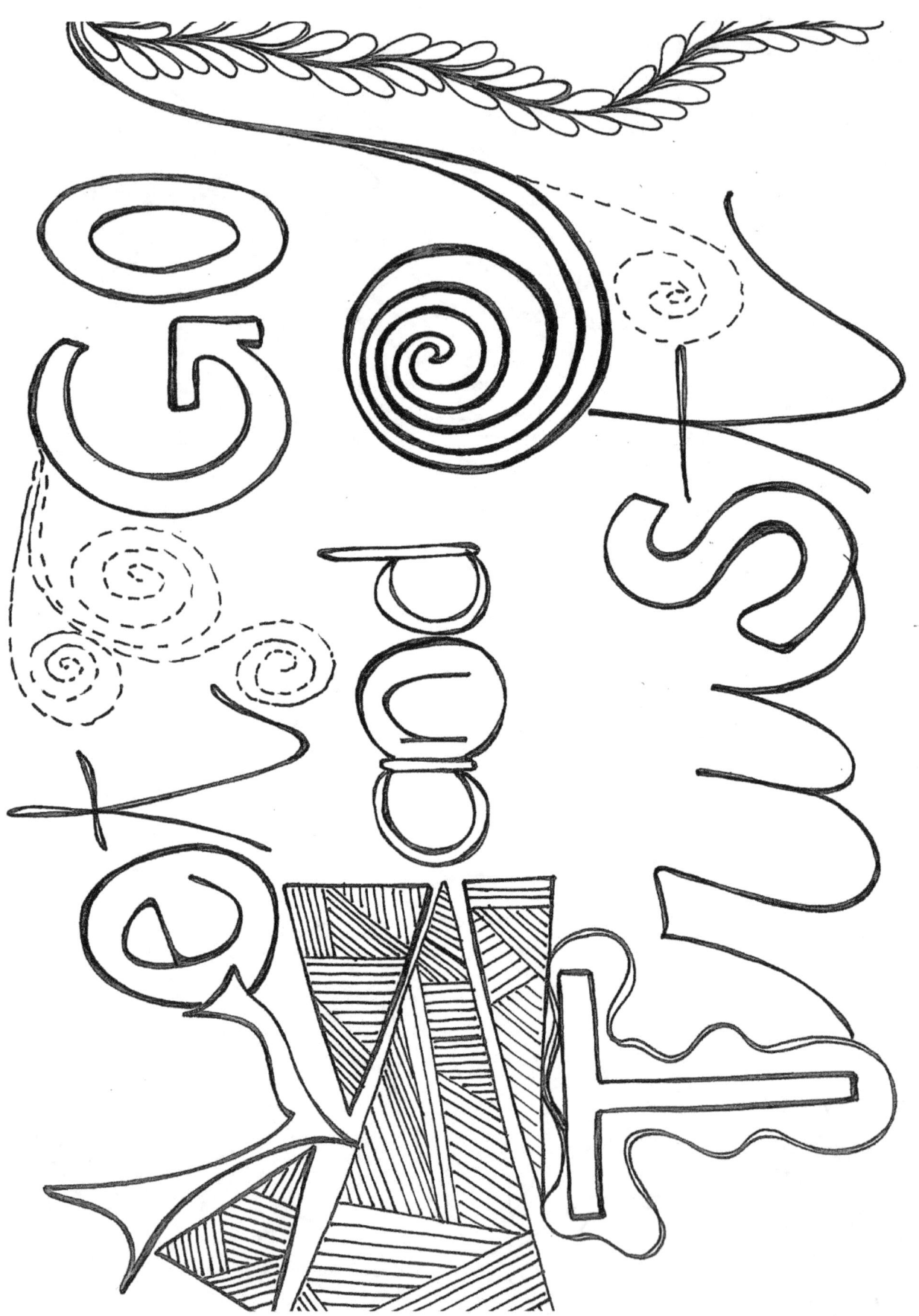

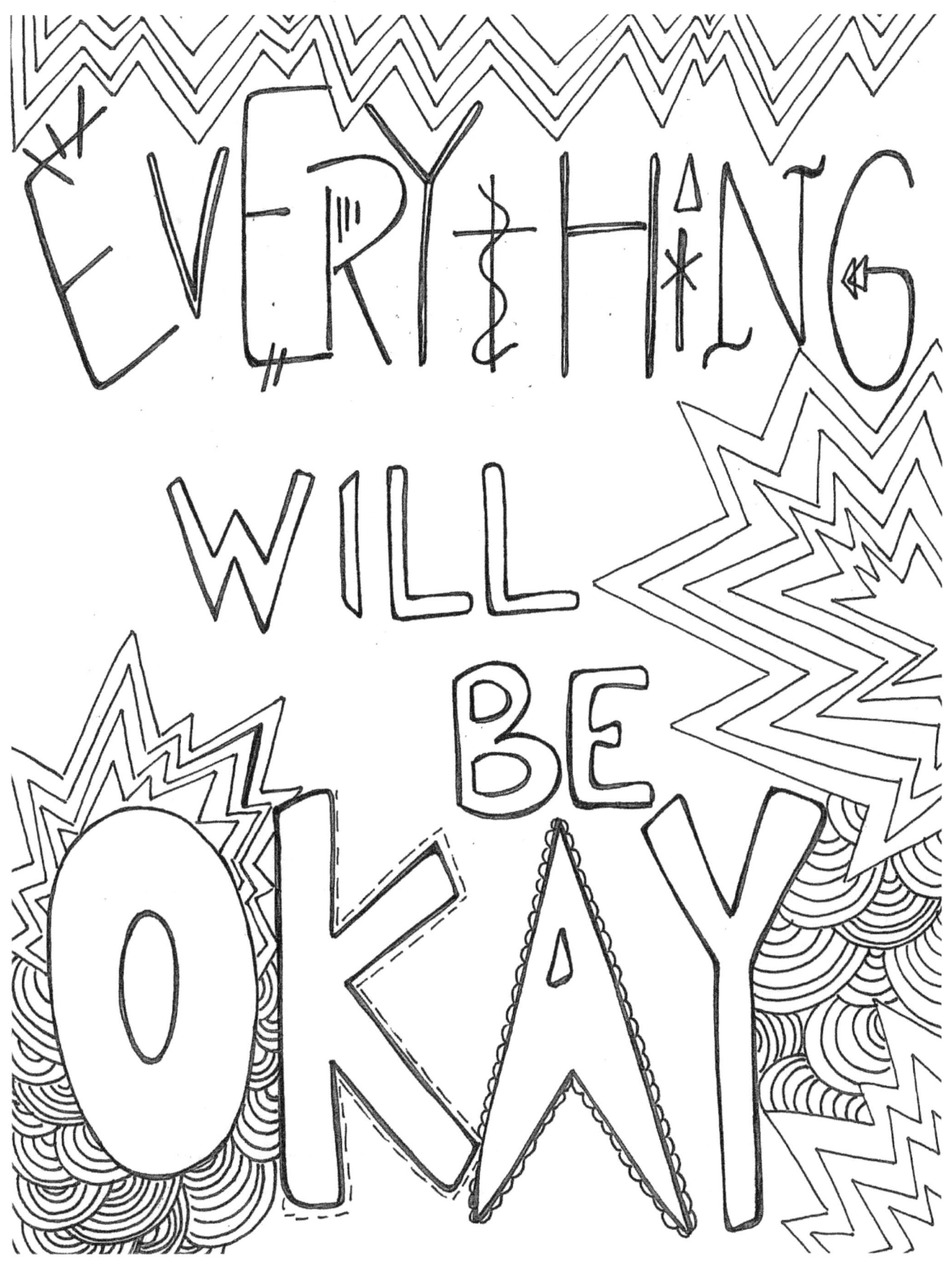

POSITIVE EXPERIENCES

Briefly write about a time or situation when you displayed the following qualities... Save your reflections for when you need a reminder!

◎ Sacrifice_____
_____

◎ Courage_____
_____

◎ Assertiveness_____
_____

◎ Love_____
_____

◎ Forgiveness_____
_____
_____

⊚ Determination _____

_____

⊚ Support _____

_____

⊚ Self-Worth _____

_____

⊚ Acceptance _____

_____

⊚ Self-Control _____

_____

⊚ Trust _____

_____

⊚ Peace _____

_____

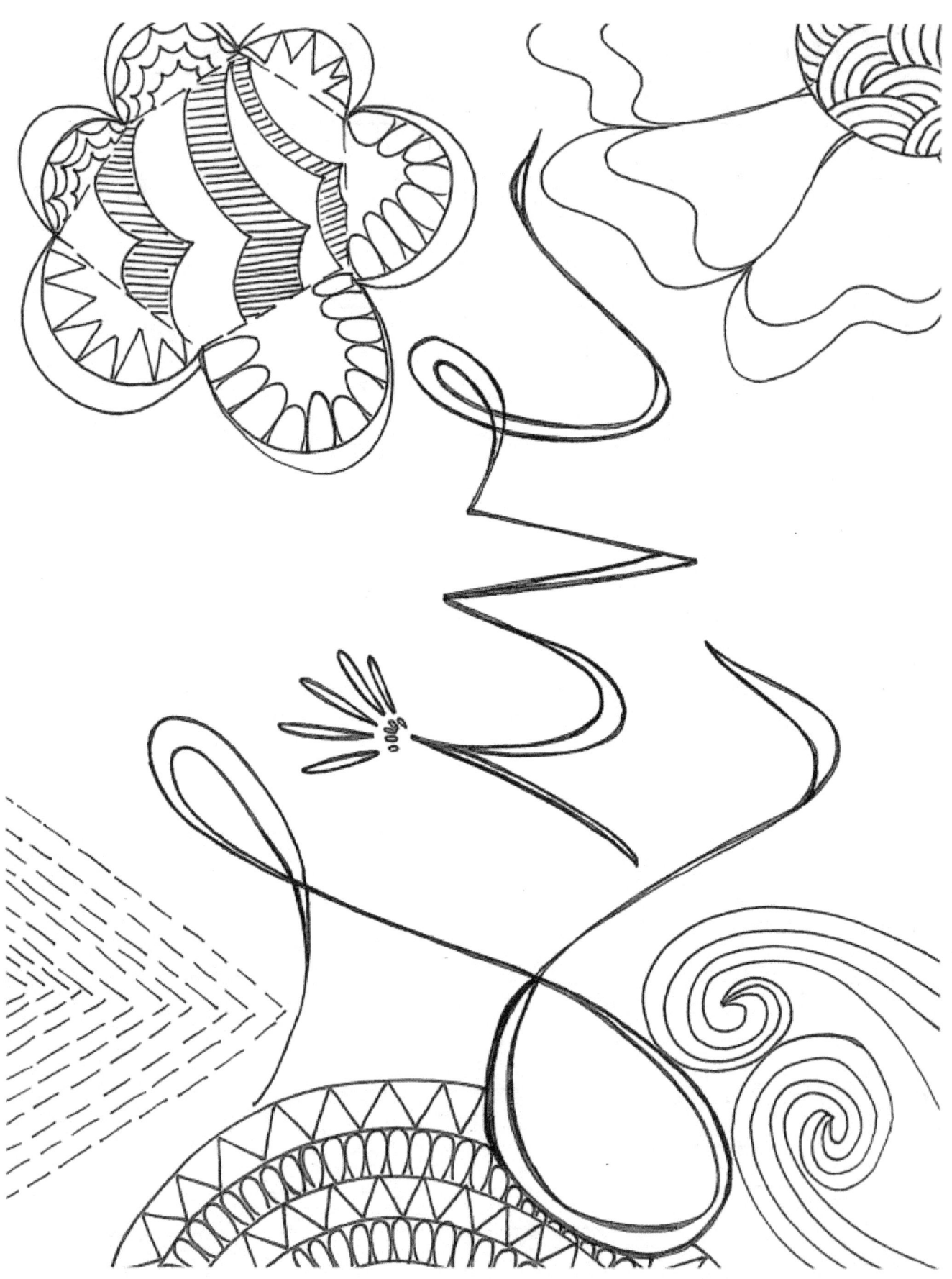

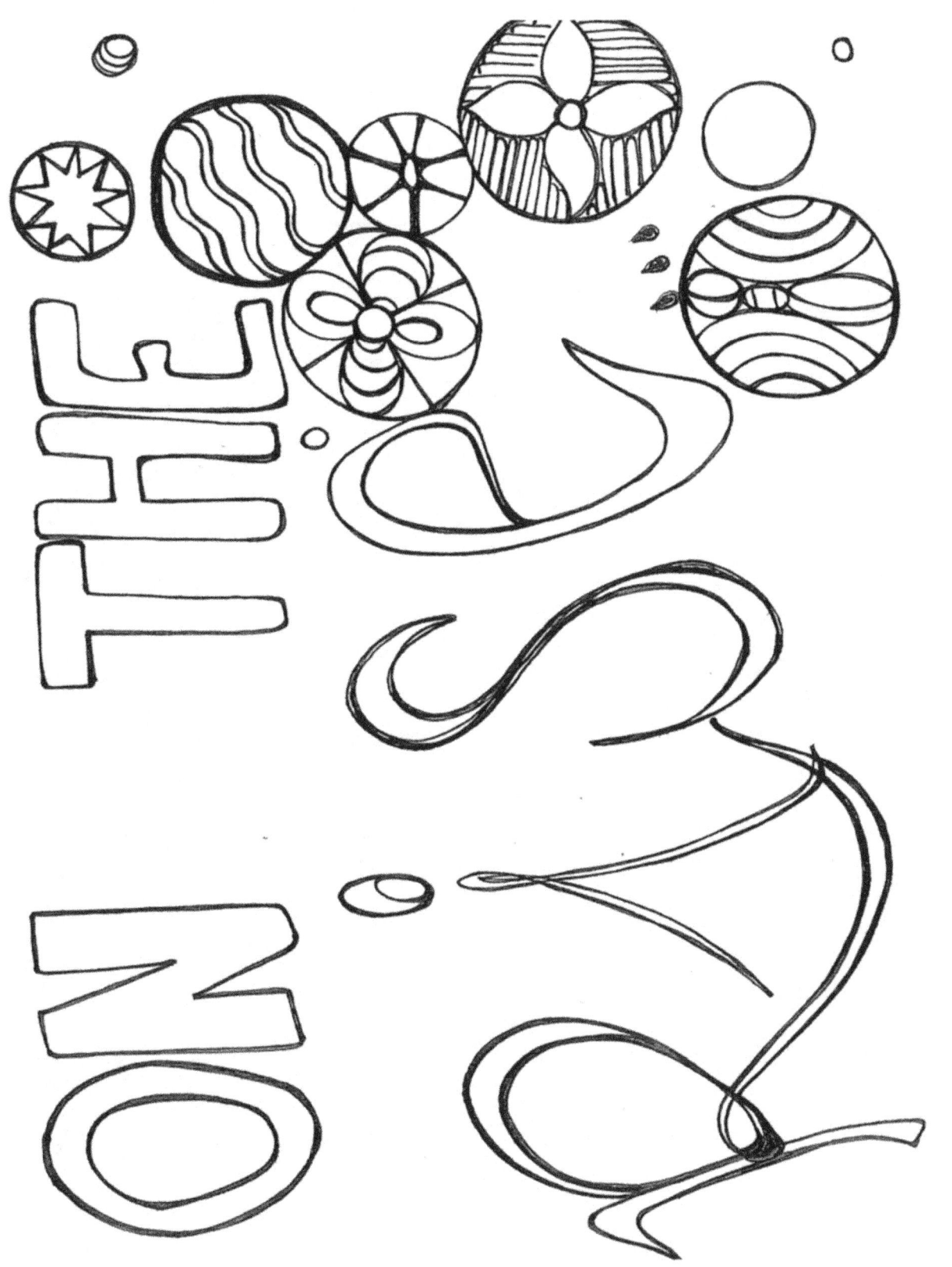

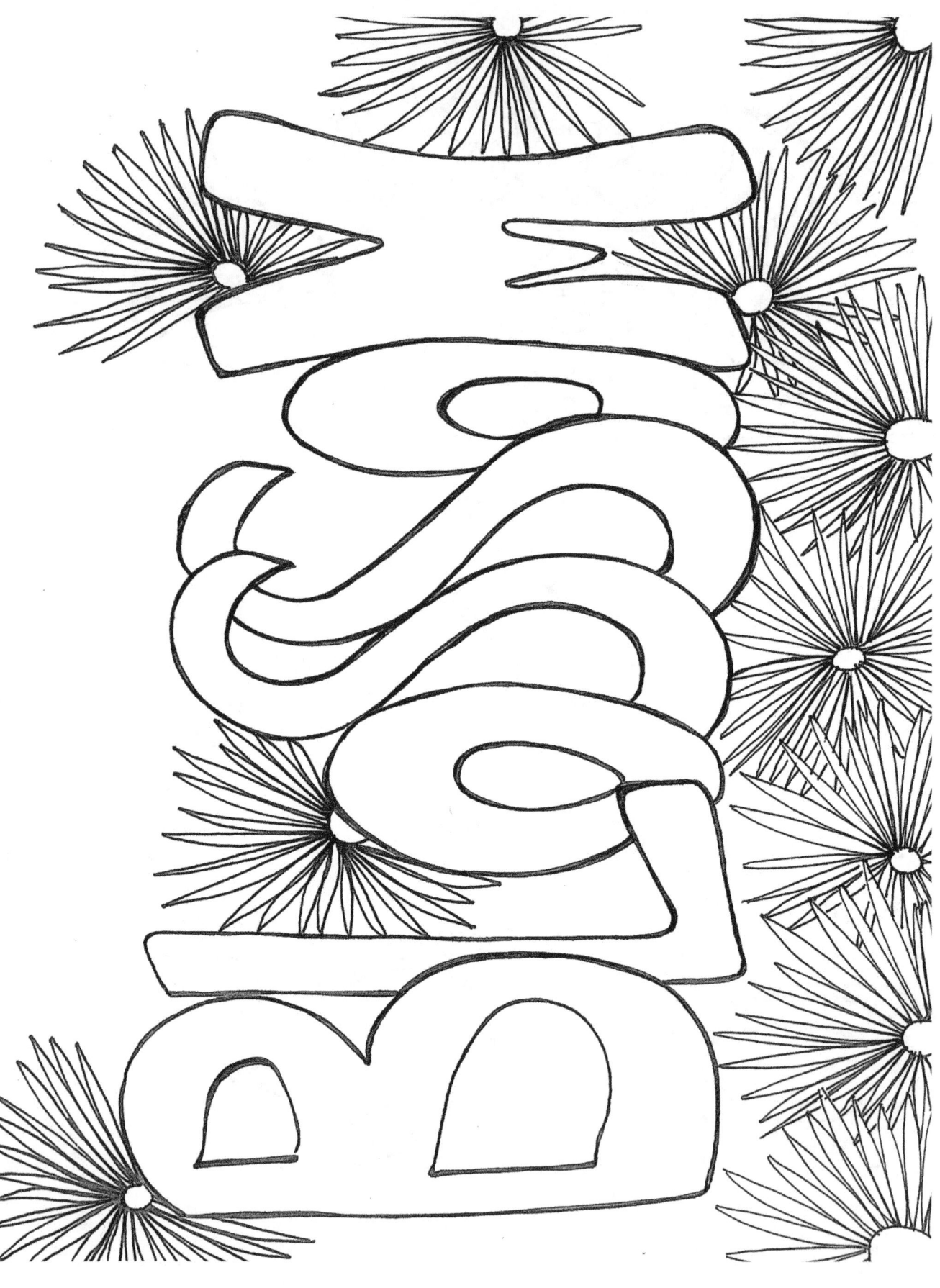

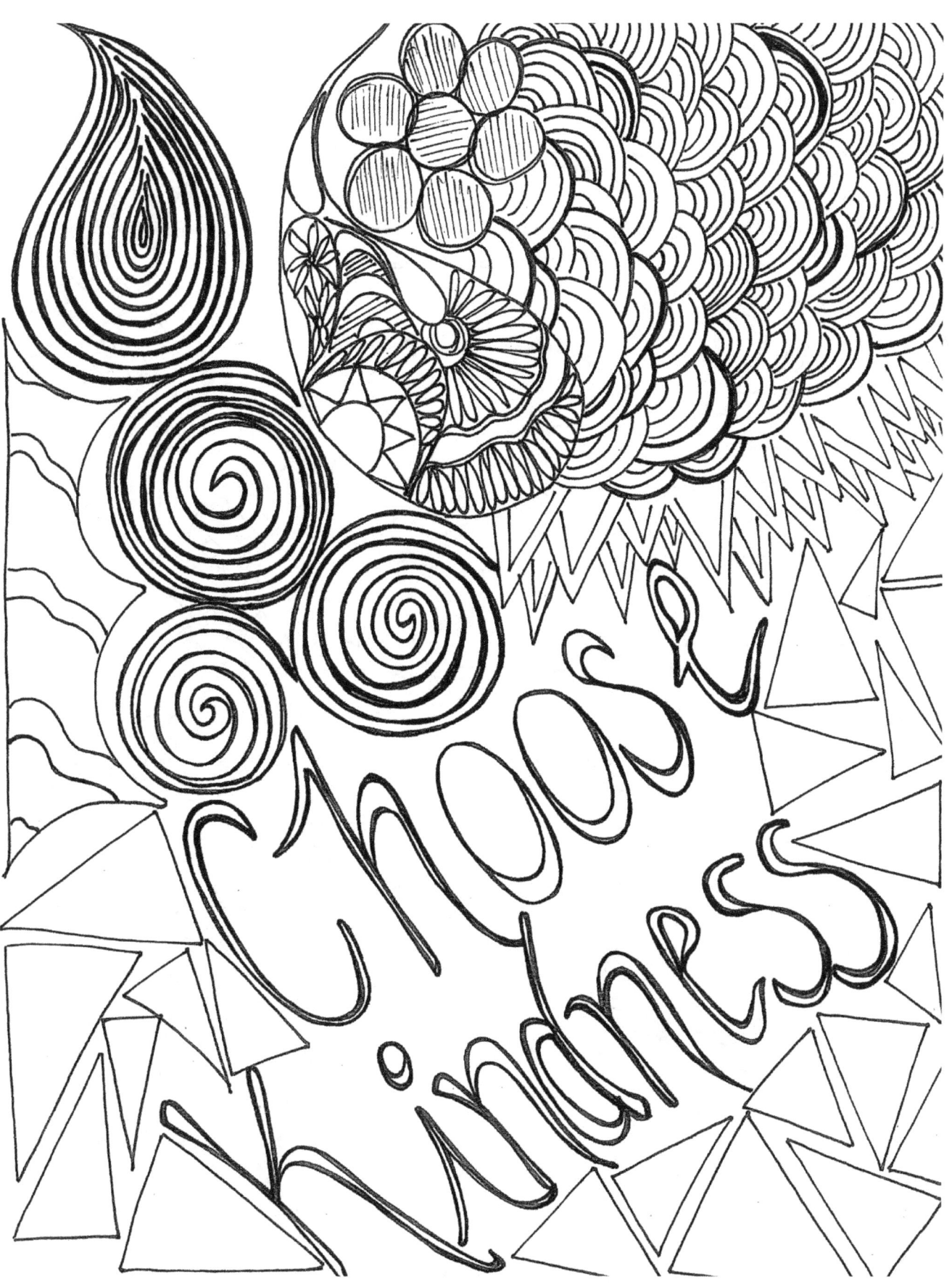

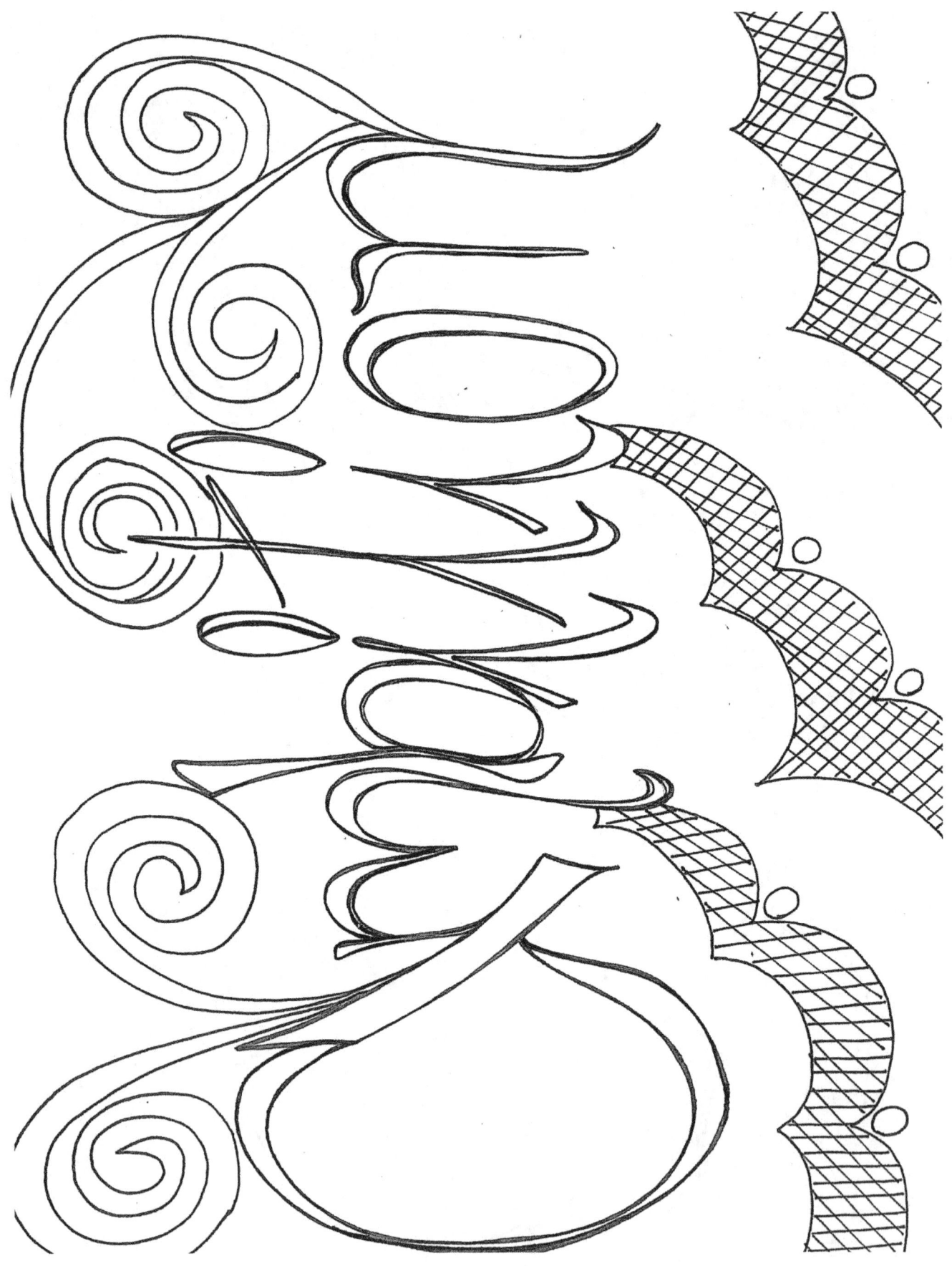

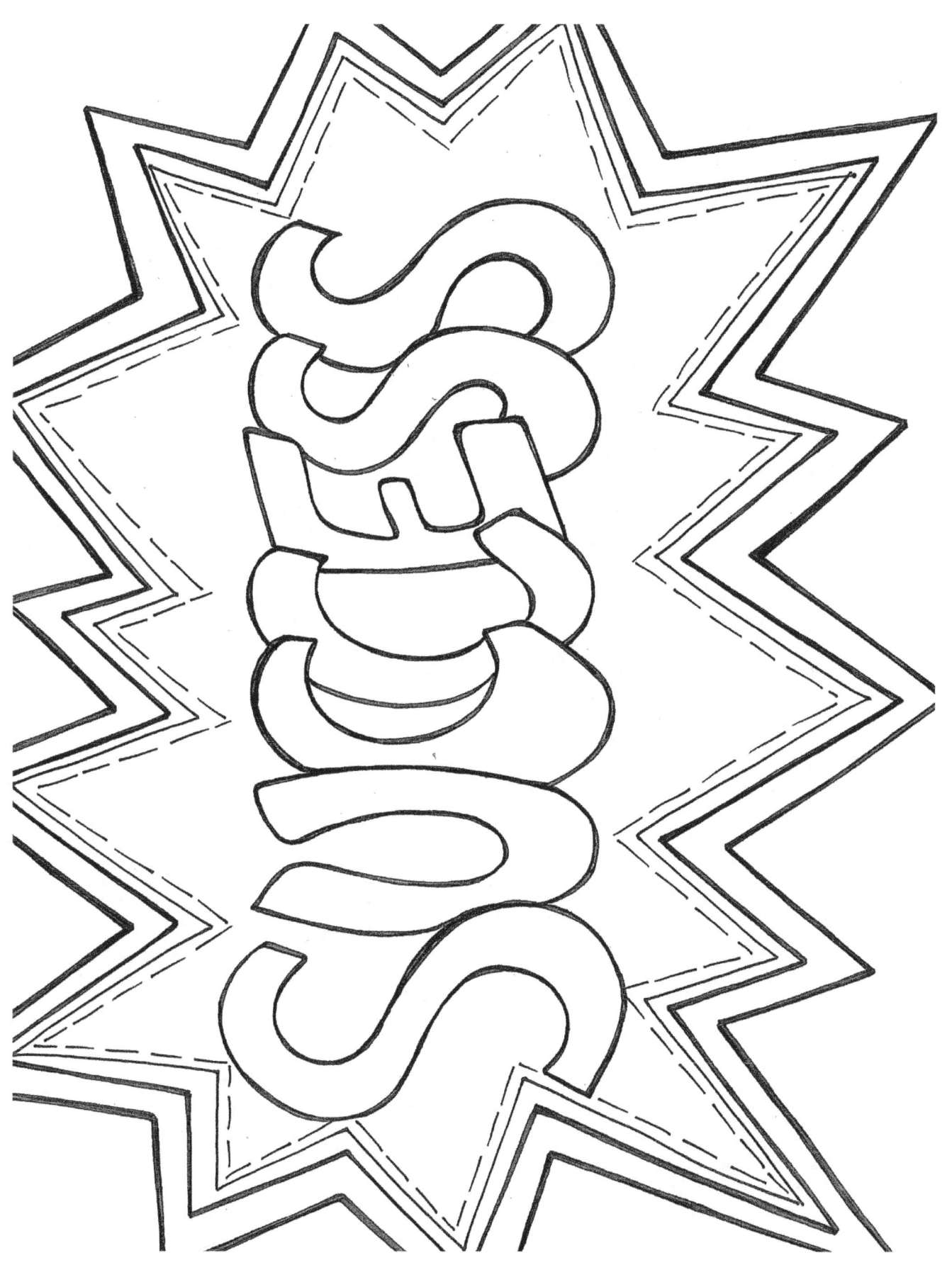

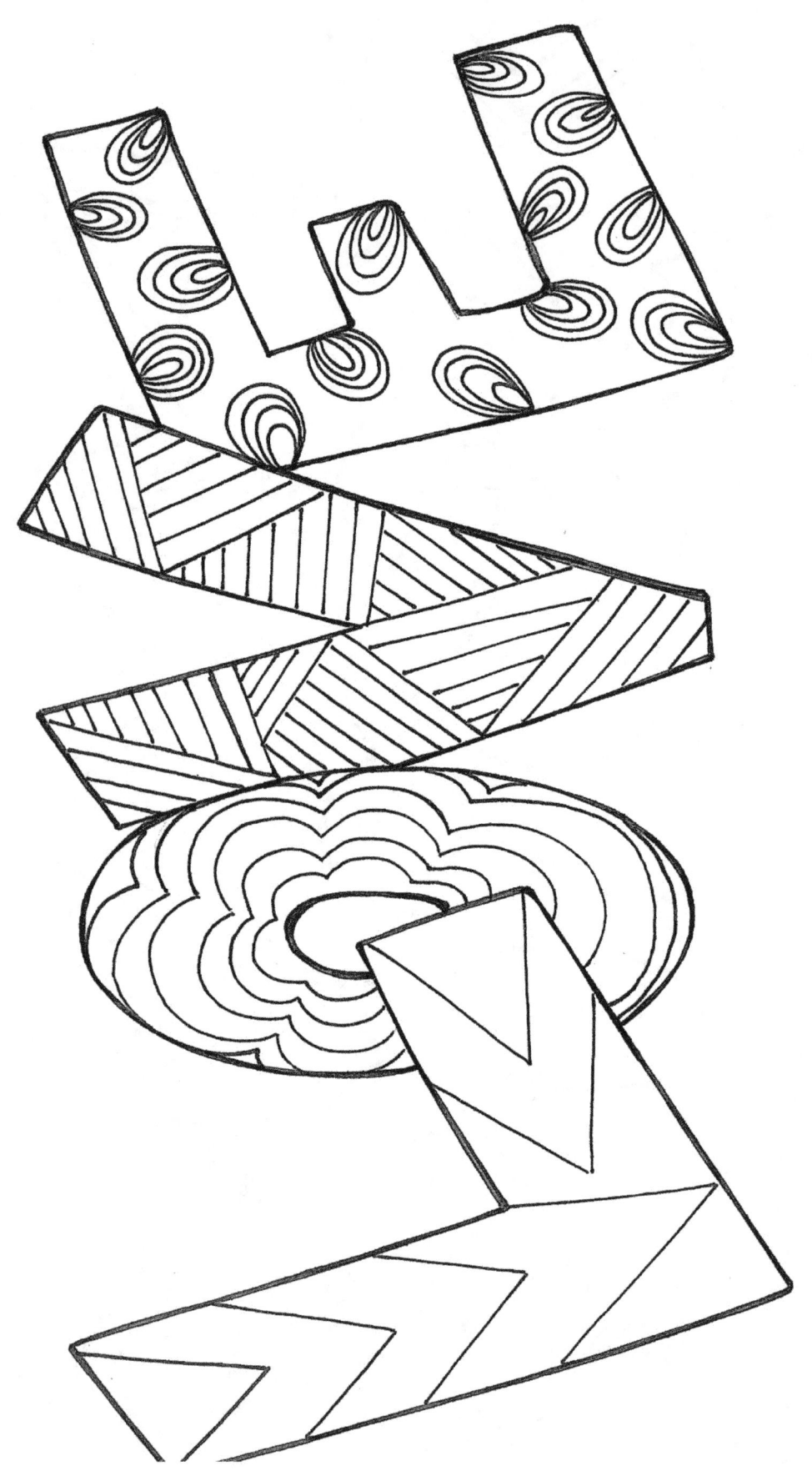

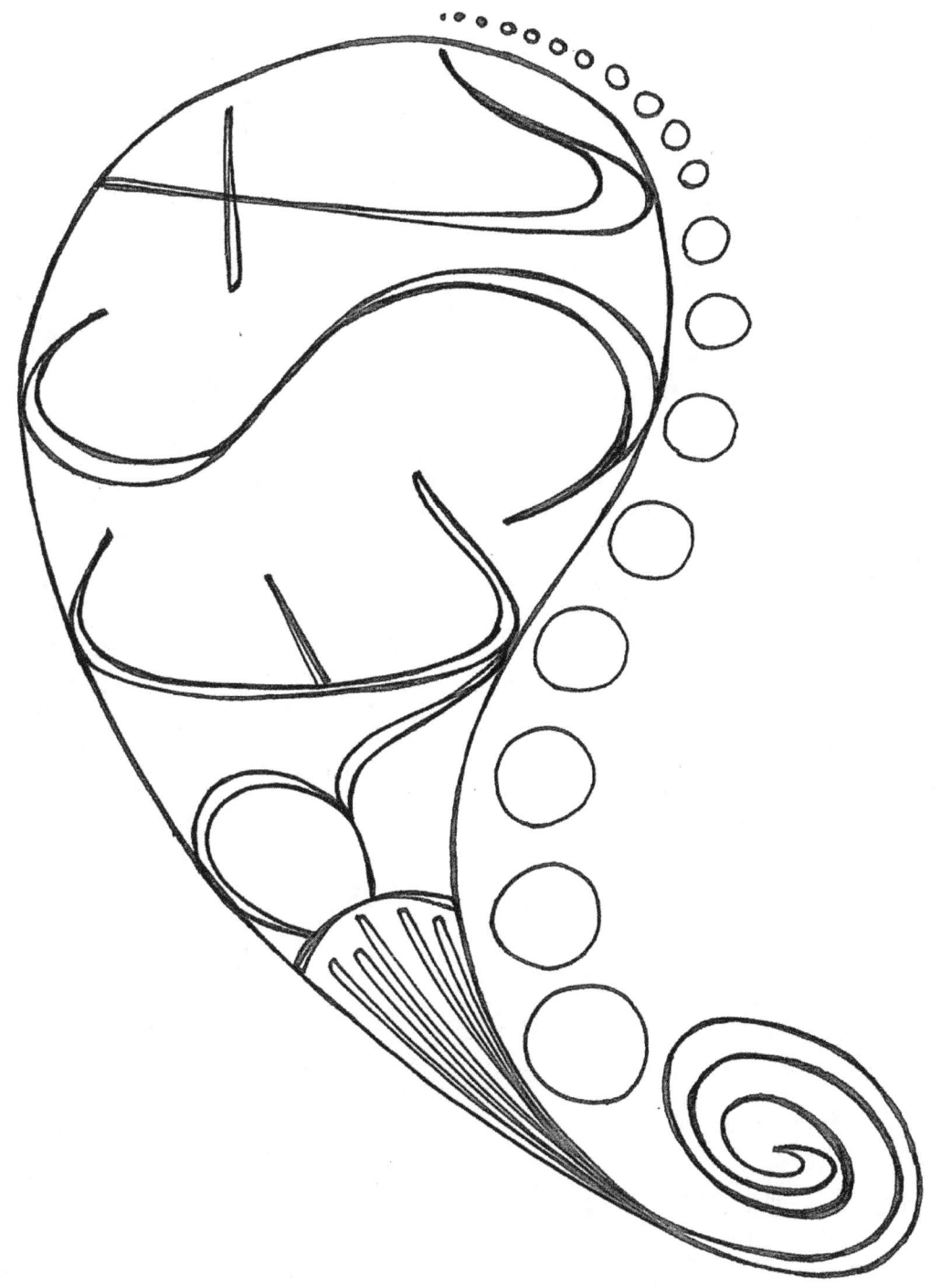

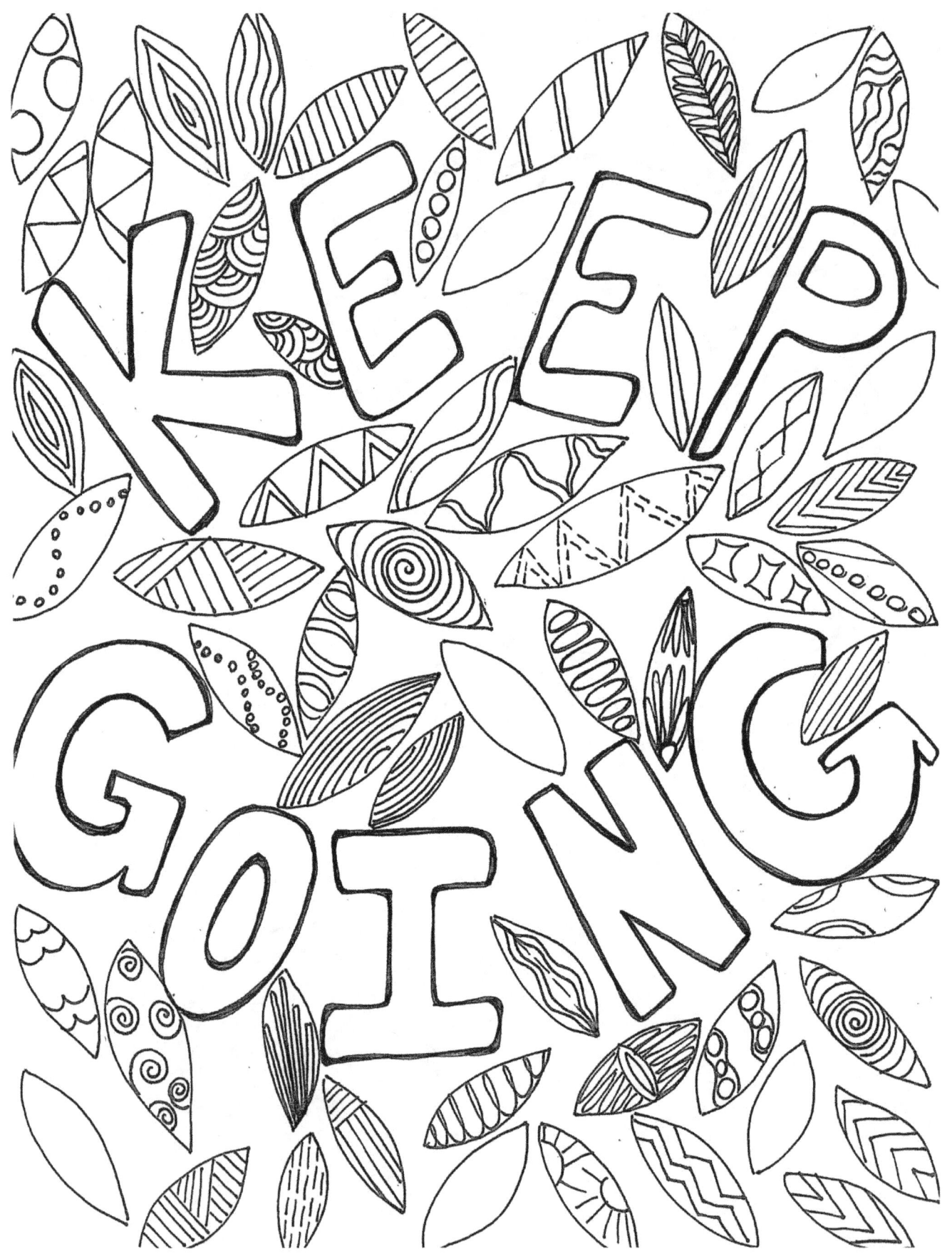

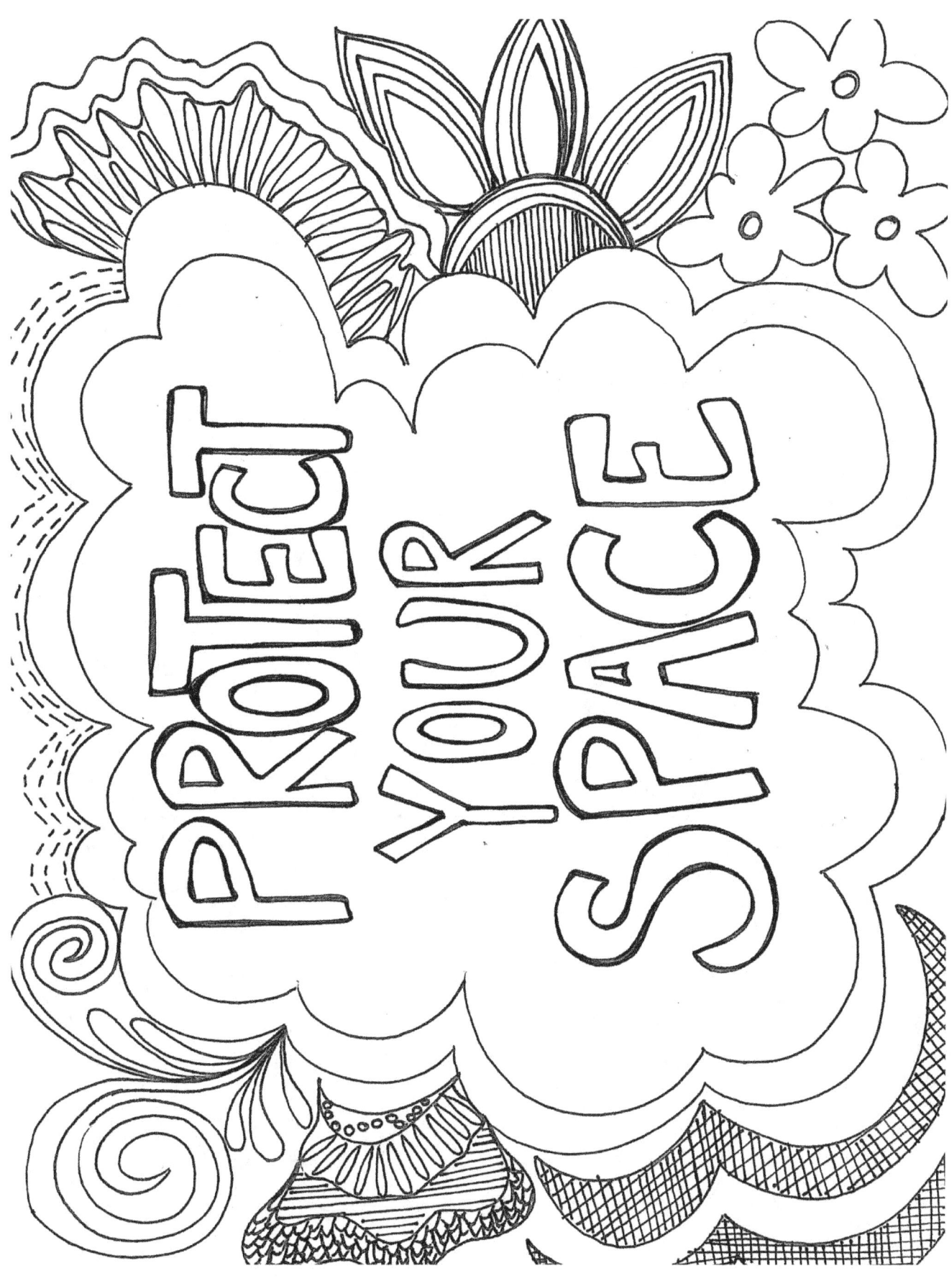

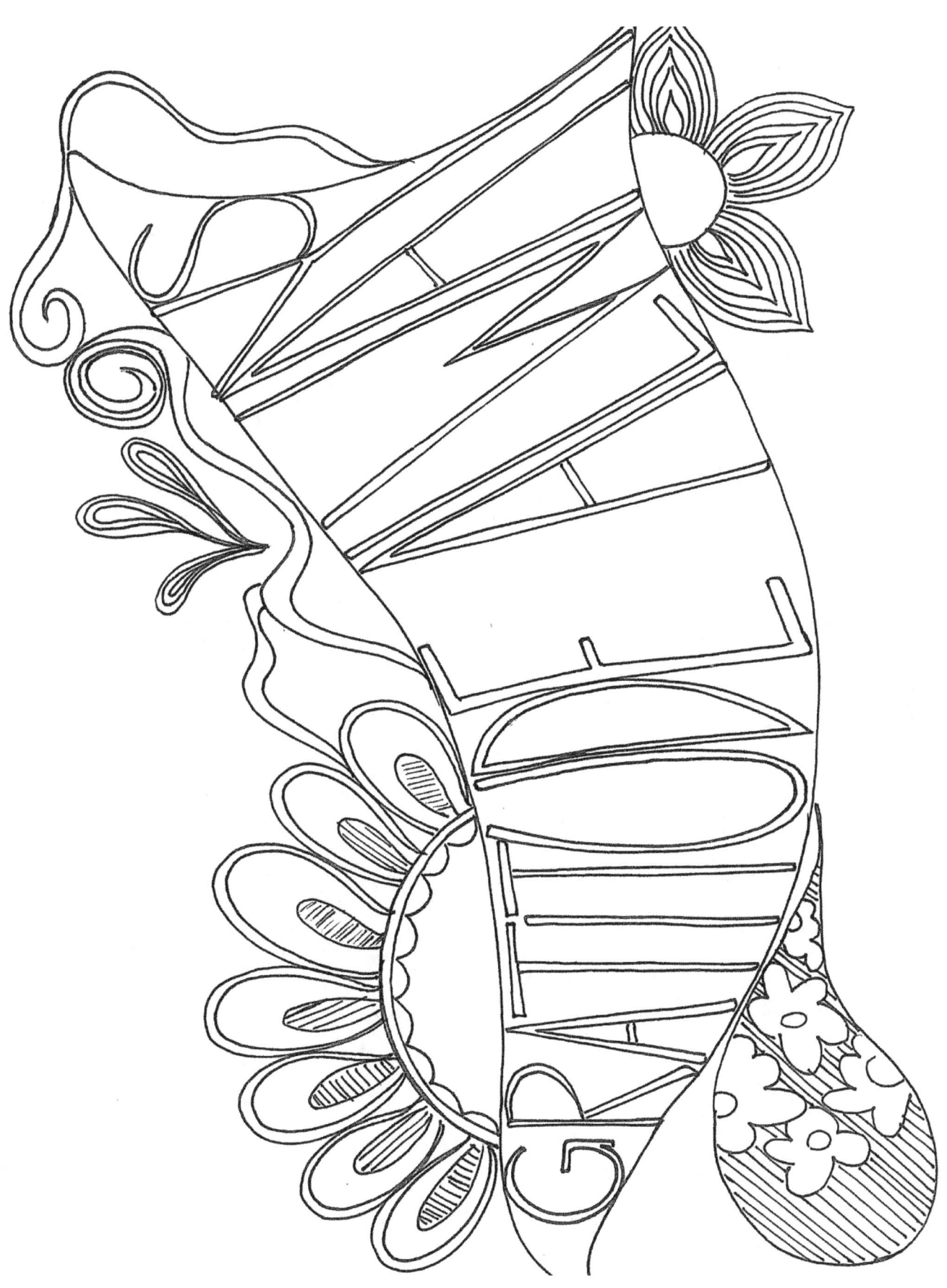

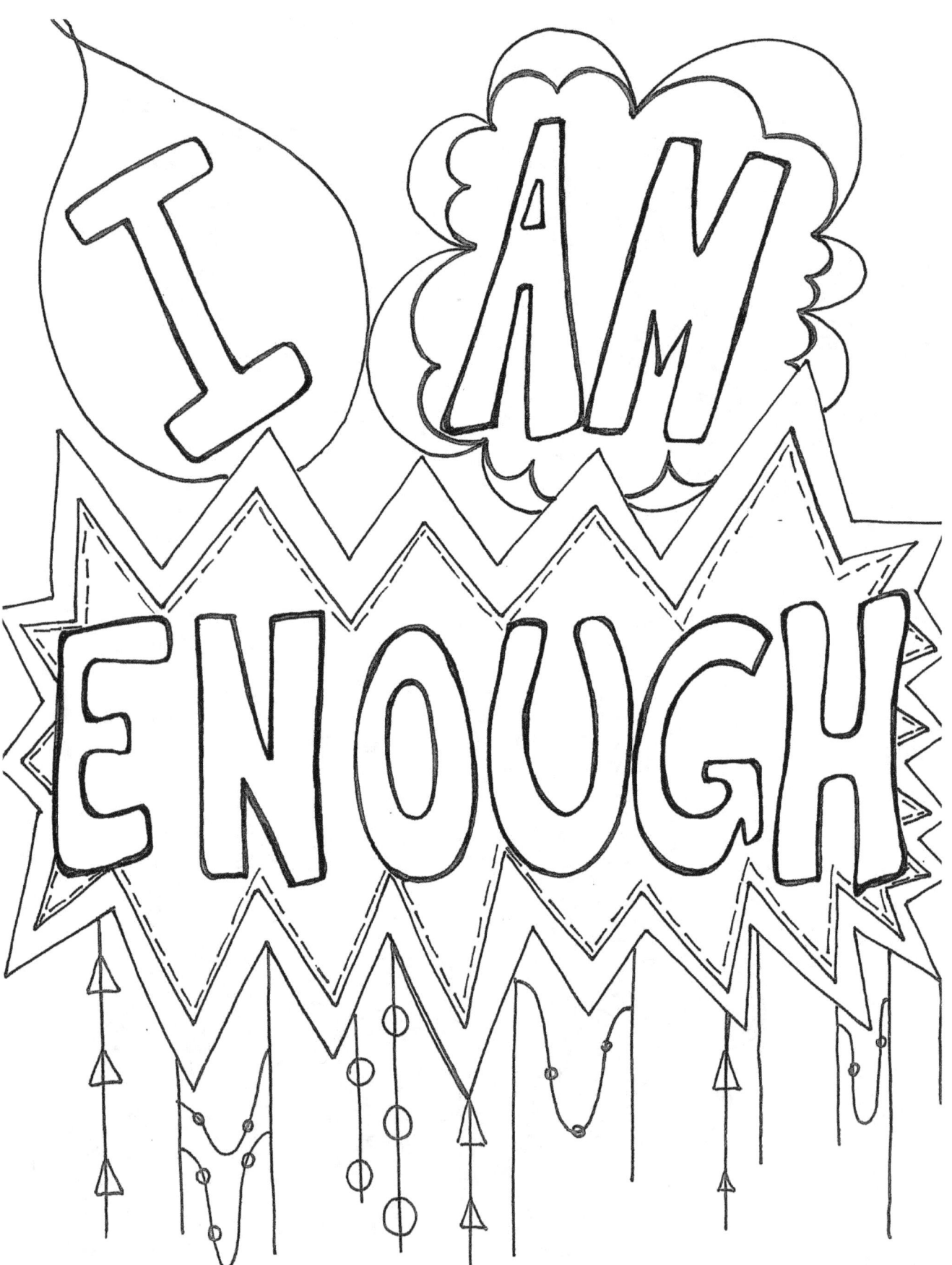

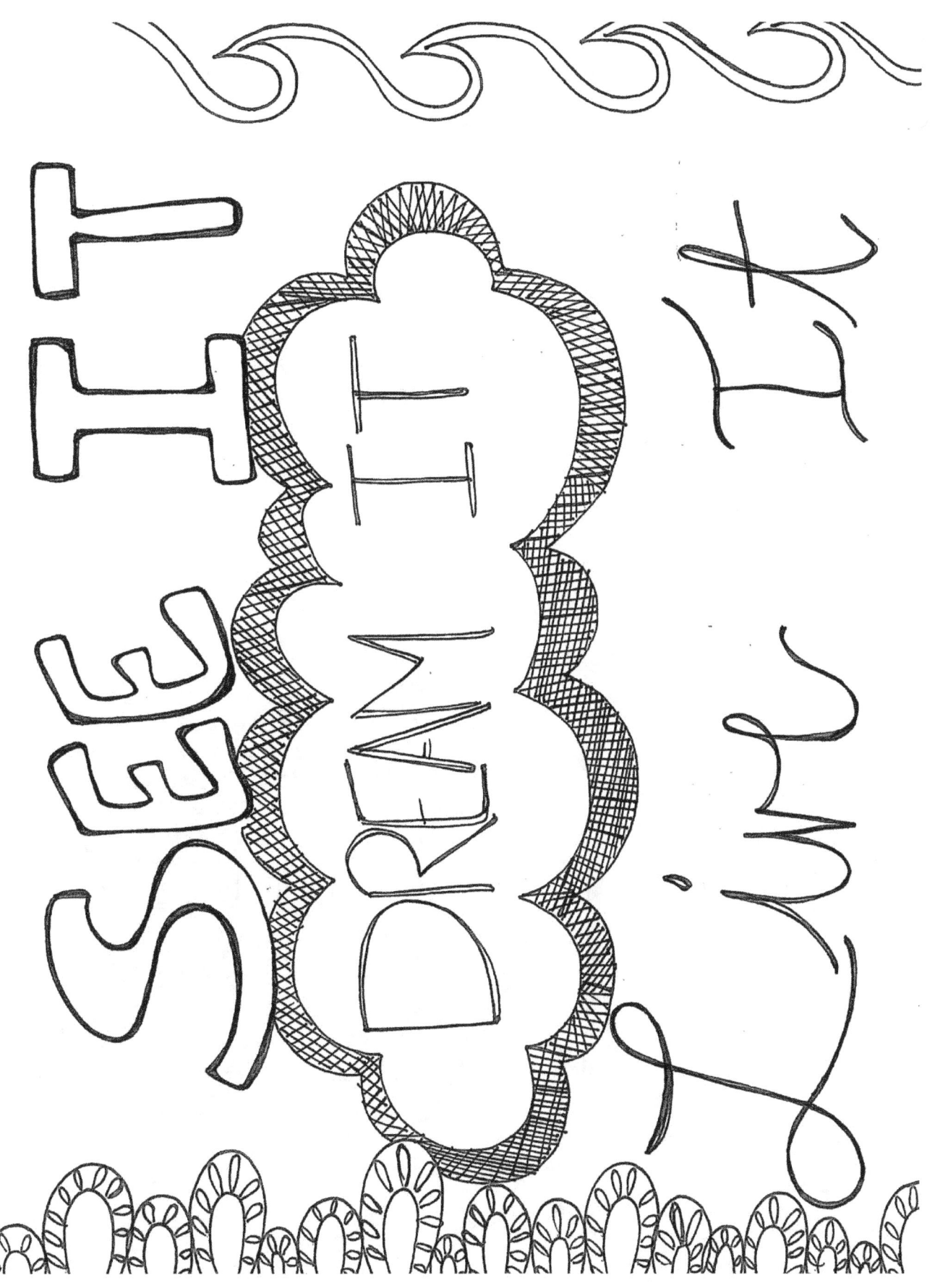

I Stand
in my
POWER

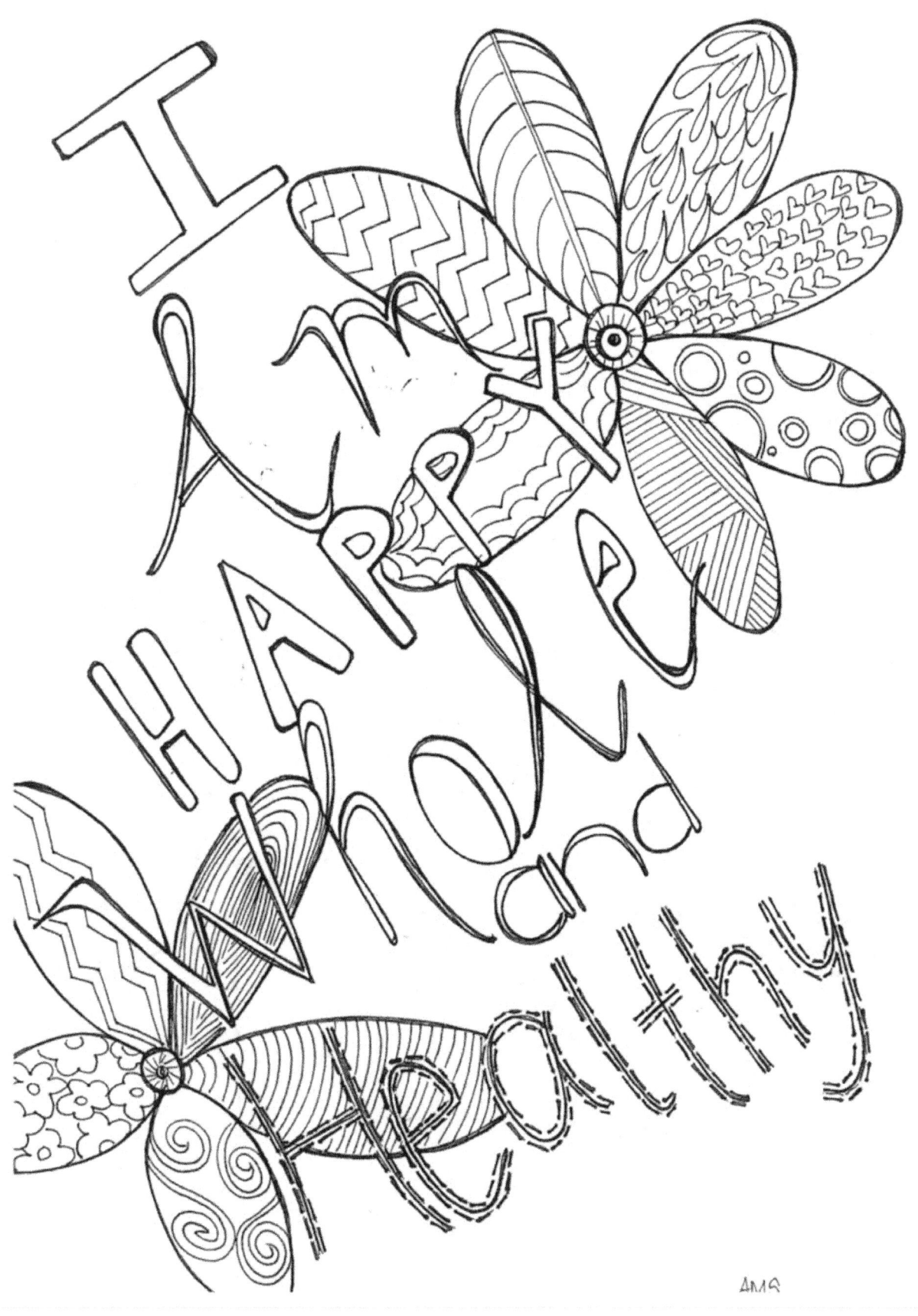

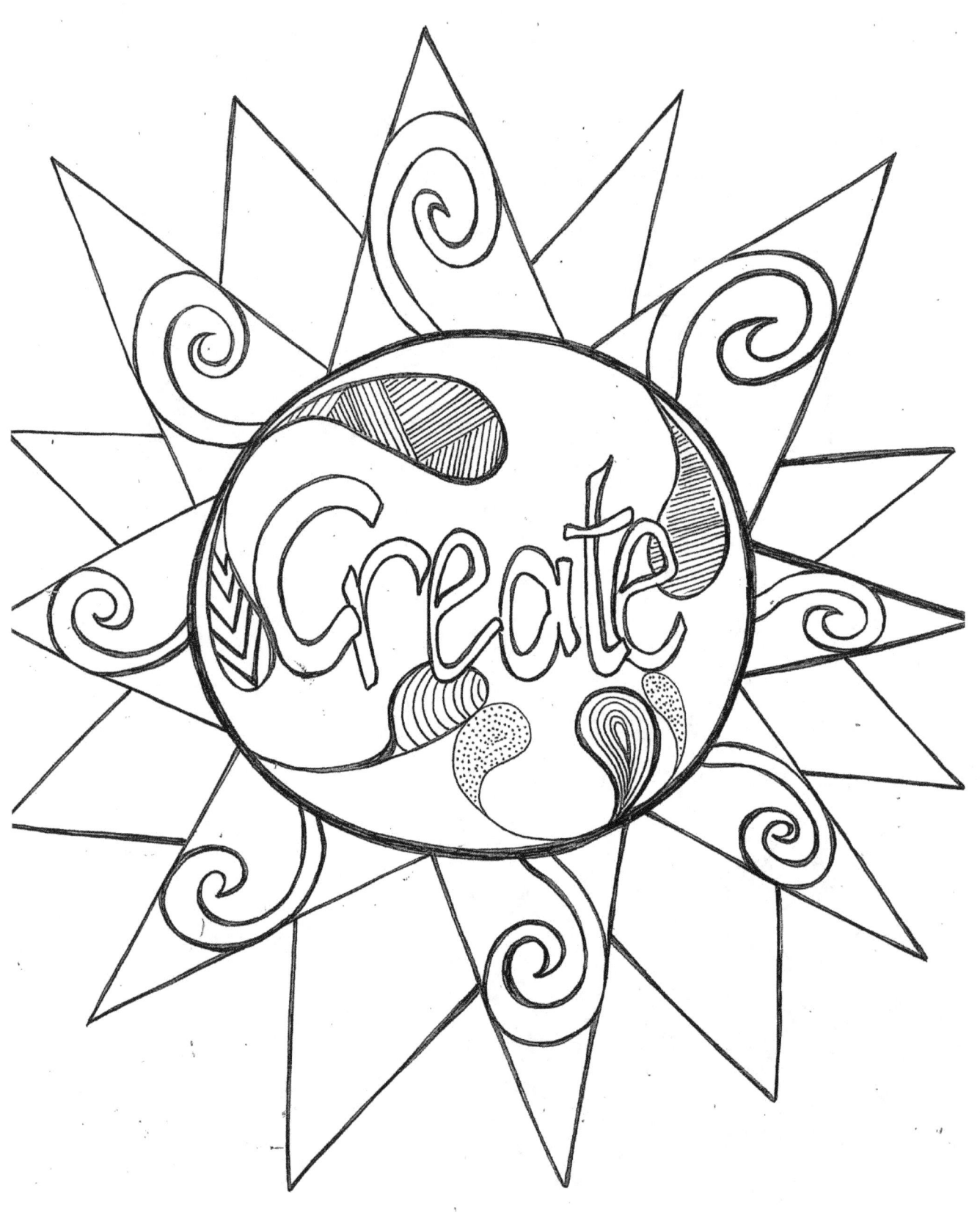

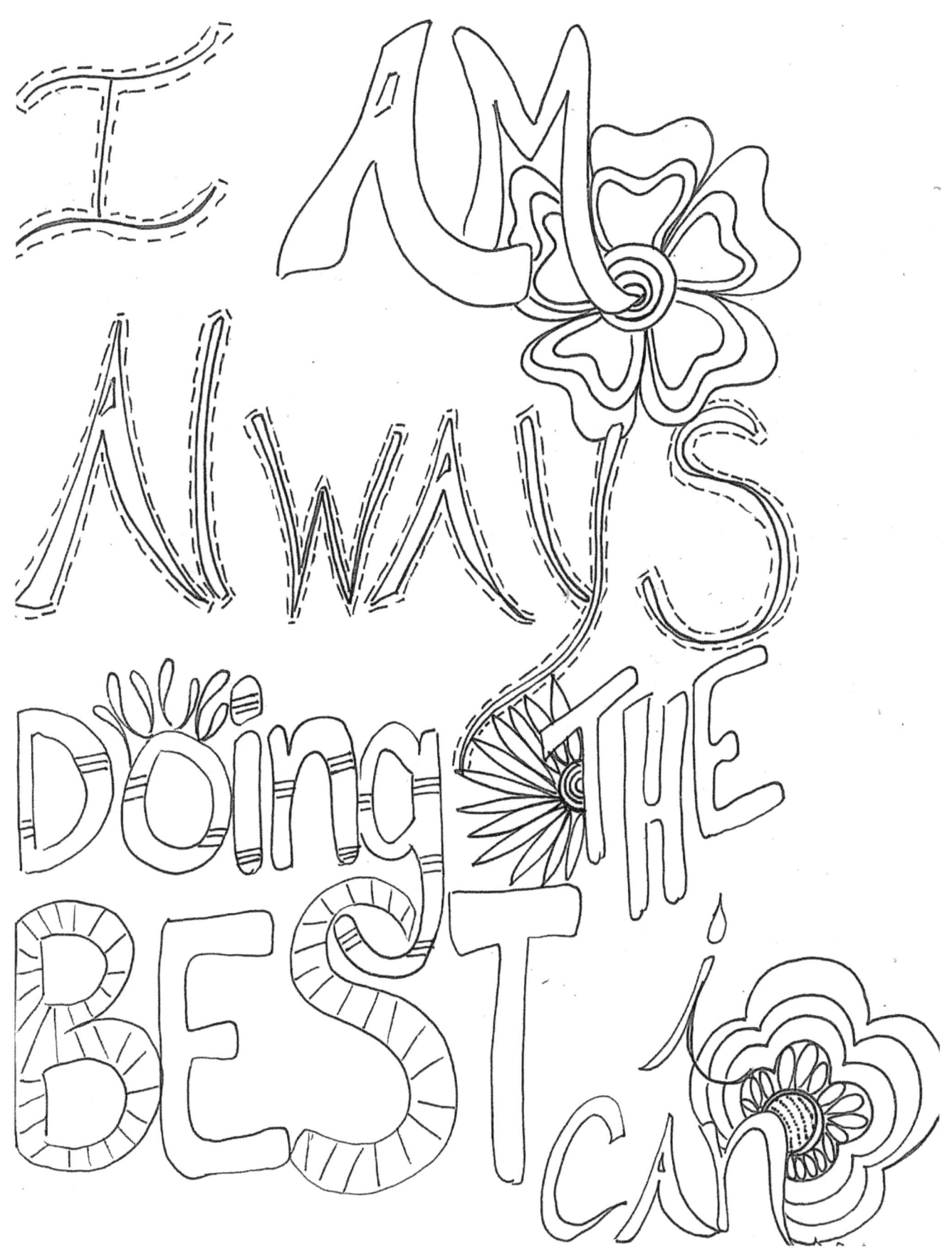

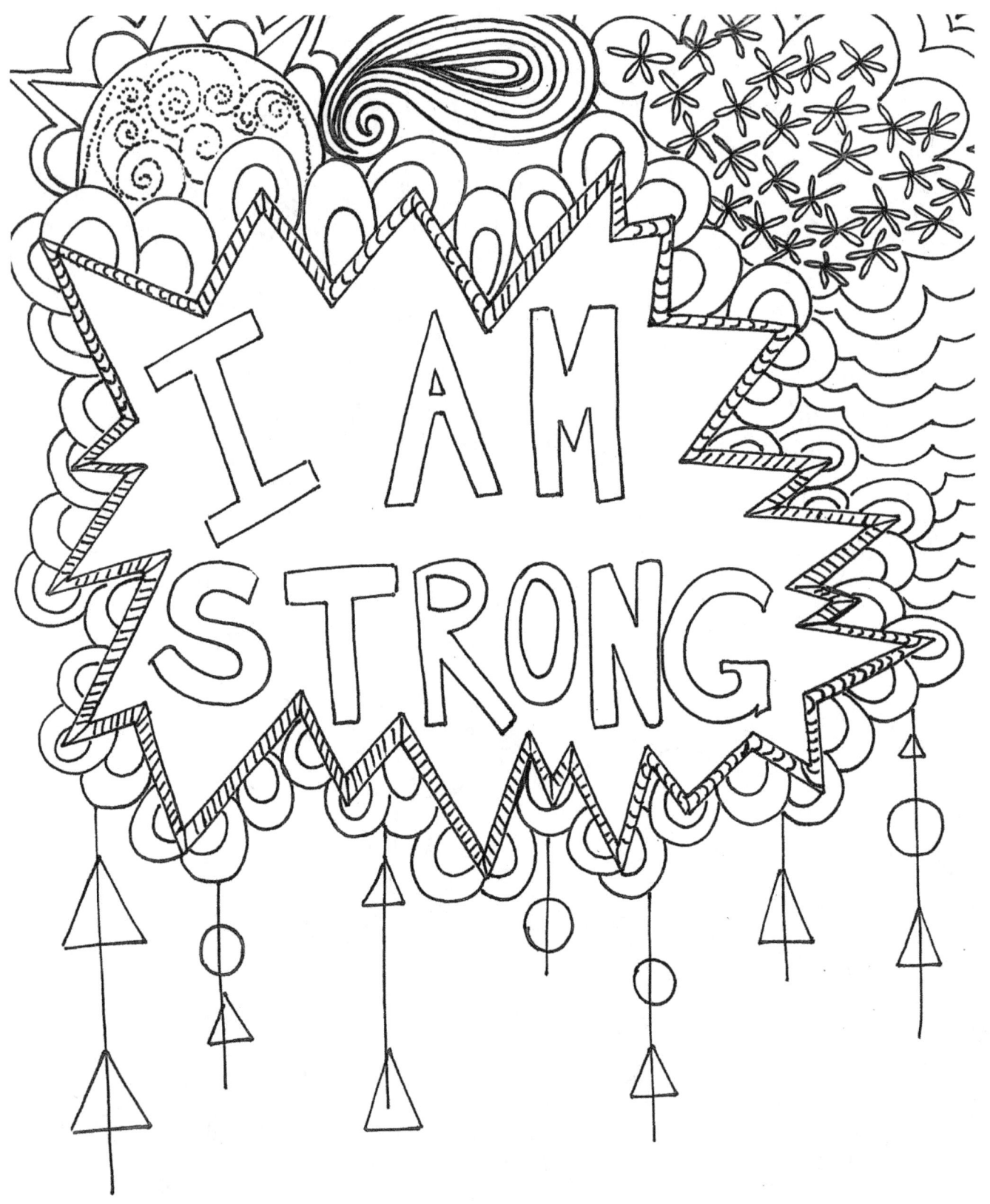